My name is

_____

I was born on

_____

I was baptized on

_____

I made my First Communion on

_____

This book was given to me by

_____

_____

Nihil Obstat: Rev. Brian E. Mahoney, S.T.L.

Imprimatur: ✠ Most Rev. Seán O'Malley, O.F.M. Cap.
Archbishop of Boston
November 10, 2004

Compiled by the Daughters of St. Paul

Illustrated by Virginia Esquinaldo

Pages 4, 11–13, 15–19, 22, 24–25, 28–37, 44–47: Maria Luisa Begnini, *Il mio primo Messalino* (Milan, Edizioni Paoline), 1990. Used with permission.

Translated by Edmund C. Lane, SSP

The English translation of the Act of Contrition from *Rite of Penance* © 1974, International Committee on English in the Liturgy, Inc. (ICEL); the English translation of the Salve Regina (Hail, Holy Queen) and the Prayer to the Guardian Angel from *A Book of Prayers* © 1982, ICEL. All rights reserved.

The English translation of the Apostles' Creed and the Doxology by the International Consultation on English Texts.

ISBN 0-8198-4843-3

Published by Pauline Books & Media, 50 Saint Pauls Avenue, Boston, MA 02130-3491. www. pauline.org.

Printed in the U.S.A.

Pauline Books & Media is the publishing house of the Daughters of St. Paul, an international congregation of women religious serving the Church with the communications media.

2 3 4 5 6 7   12 11 10 09 08

Contents

My Prayers

The Liturgical Year

My Prayers

God speaks to you at home, at school,
when you're with friends, everywhere.
In the silence of your heart,
    he speaks to you
about you, about those you love,
about everyone in the world.

You can pray alone or when you
    are with others,
in church, at home, or in religion class.
You don't need to use a lot of words,
but it is very important to want to speak
    to God
and to listen to him as your friend.

Basic Prayers

The Sign of the Cross

In the name of the Father,
and of the Son,
and of the Holy Spirit. Amen.

Our Father

Our Father, who art in heaven,
hallowed be thy name.
Thy kingdom come,
thy will be done on earth
as it is in heaven.
Give us this day
our daily bread,
and forgive us our trespasses,
as we forgive those
who trespass against us.
And lead us not into temptation,
but deliver us from evil. Amen.

Hail Mary

Hail Mary, full of grace,
the Lord is with you.
Blessed are you among women,
and blessed is the fruit of your womb,
    Jesus.
Holy Mary, Mother of God,
pray for us sinners
now and at the hour of our death.
Amen.

Glory

Glory to the Father
and to the Son,
and to the Holy Spirit.
As it was in the beginning,
is now,
and will be for ever.
Amen.

Prayer to the Guardian Angel

Angel sent by God to guide me,
be my light and walk beside me;
be my guardian and protect me;
on the paths of life direct me.

The Apostles' Creed

I believe in God, the Father almighty,
    creator of heaven and earth.
I believe in Jesus Christ, his only Son,
        our Lord.
    He was conceived by the power of the
        Holy Spirit
    and born of the Virgin Mary.
    He suffered under Pontius Pilate,
        was crucified, died, and was buried.
    He descended to the dead.
    On the third day he rose again.
    He ascended into heaven,
        and is seated at the right hand
            of the Father.
    He will come again to judge the
        living and the dead.
I believe in the Holy Spirit,
    the holy catholic Church,
    the communion of saints,
    the forgiveness of sins,
    the resurrection of the body,
    and the life everlasting. Amen.

Act of Faith

O my God,
I firmly believe that you are one God
in three Divine Persons,
Father, Son, and Holy Spirit;
I believe that your Divine Son became
    man
and died for our sins,
and that he will come again
to judge the living and the dead.
I believe these
and all the truths
which the holy Catholic Church teaches,
because you have revealed them
who can neither deceive nor be deceived.

Act of Hope

O my God,
relying on your infinite goodness
    and promises,
I hope to obtain pardon of my sins,
the help of your grace,
and life everlasting,
through the merits of Jesus Christ,
my Lord and Redeemer.

Act of Love

O my God,
I love you above all things,
with my whole heart and soul,
because you are all good and worthy of
    all love.
I love my neighbor as myself
    for the love of you.
I forgive all who have injured me
and ask pardon of all whom I
    have injured.

Act of Contrition

My God,
I am sorry for my sins with all my heart.
In choosing to do wrong
and failing to do good,
I have sinned against you
whom I should love above all things.
I firmly intend, with your help,
to do penance,
to sin no more,
and to avoid whatever leads me to sin.

Our Savior Jesus Christ
suffered and died for us.
In his name, my God, have mercy.

In the Morning

The city, the country, the world is
    waking up.
It's coming to life.
People are going to work.

I am getting up, too, and like many
    other Christians,
I make the Sign of the Cross.
I remember that God is with me.
Jesus invites me to be his friend through-
    out the day.

I Adore You

I adore you, my God,
and I love you with all my heart.
I thank you for having created me.
I thank you for having made me
    a Christian.
I thank you for having kept me safe
    during the night.
I offer you everything I will do today.
Help me to be good and to obey your
    holy will.
Bless me, my parents, and everyone I
    love. Amen.

I Praise You, O Lord

You have made the sun and the moon,
the animals that live on land, the birds
    and the fish.
You have made us a little less than the
    angels.
You have given us a mind with which
    to think.
You have made us able to love.
You have given us the desire to do
    good things.

During the Day

A Prayer for Peace

This prayer will help you to bring love and peace to others. In this way you will help make the world a more beautiful place in which to live.

Lord,
make me an instrument of your peace.
Where they is hatred, let me bring love.
Where there is injury, let me bring
    pardon.
Where there is doubt, let me bring faith.
Where there is despair, let me bring
    hope.
Where there is darkness, let me bring
    light.
Where there is sadness, let me bring joy.

St. Francis of Assisi

Prayer Before Meals

Bless us, O Lord,
and these your gifts
which we are about
to receive from your bounty,
through Christ our Lord. Amen.

Prayer After Meals

We give you thanks,
for all your benefits,
O loving God,
you who live and reign
for ever. Amen.

Think about how you have spent the day.
Thank God for the many gifts he has
given you.
Ask God to forgive all your faults.

I Adore You

I adore you, my God,
and I love you with all my heart.
Thank you for having created me.
Thank you for having made me a
    Christian.
Thank you for having watched over
    me today.
Accept the good things I have done, and
forgive me for anything I have
    done wrong.
Take care of me while I'm sleeping.
Bless me, my parents, and everyone I
    love. Amen.

Ask God to protect all the people in the
world this night.

Lord,
watch over, help, and protect everybody
    in my house,
my neighborhood, my city, and the
    whole world. Amen.

Other Prayers

For My Mother and Father

Lord, I thank you for having given me
    good parents.
My mother and father do so much
    for me.
Please keep them with me for a long,
    long time.
Help me to make them happy.
Let us always love and understand
    each other
just as Jesus, Mary, and Joseph did in
    their house at Nazareth.
Amen.

For My Friends

Thank you, Lord, for my friends.
Thank you for all the good they do.
Thank you for their kindness to me.
Help me to be a good friend to everyone.
Make me always willing to share
what I have with others. Amen.

For All Children Like Me

Lord, I pray
that all children may be loved and
    respected.
I pray that all children may have a
    family
that welcomes them and cares for them.
I pray that all children may know and
    love you. Amen.

For the Church

Lord, I pray for all the people
who make up your Church:
the Pope, the bishops, priests, brothers,
    sisters,
grownups, teenagers, and little children.
Help us all to be signs of your love.
Help us to tell everyone the good news
that you are alive and with us today.
    Amen.

For Those Who Have Died

Eternal rest grant to them, Lord.
And let perpetual light shine on them.
May they rest in peace. Amen.

For All Who Are Suffering

Lord, help all people who are alone or
    sick.
Make them feel the power of your
    presence and your love.
Help me, too, to do something for them.
    Amen.

The Rosary

How to Pray the Rosary

1. Make the Sign of the Cross and pray the Apostles' Creed.

2. Pray one Our Father.

3. Pray three Hail Marys.

4. Pray one Glory to the Father.

7.

5. Announce the first mystery and pray one Our Father.

6. Pray ten Hail Marys.

3.

4.

2.

6.

5.

1.

In the prayer called the Rosary we remember the most important events (or mysteries) in the lives of Jesus and his mother Mary.

By thinking about these twenty special events that brought joy, light, sorrow, and glory to Jesus and Mary, we want to honor them and show them our love. When we pray the Rosary, Mary also prays to Jesus her Son for us!

7. Pray one Glory to the Father.

Repeat steps 5–7 for all five mysteries. At the end of the Rosary you can pray the Hail, Holy Queen.

The Joyful Mysteries

When we pray the Rosary on Mondays and Saturdays, we think about the birth of Jesus and the first years of his life.

1. The angel announces to Mary that she is to become the Mother of Jesus. Mary's heart is filled with happiness.
2. Mary visits her cousin Elizabeth. She stays to help her for several months until Elizabeth's baby is born.
3. Mary gives birth to Jesus. She tenderly wraps him in swaddling clothes and lays him in a manger.
4. Mary and Joseph bring Jesus to the Temple and present him as a gift to God.
5. Having searched three days for twelve-year-old Jesus, Mary and Joseph find him in the Temple in Jerusalem listening to the teachers of the law and asking them questions.

The Mysteries of Light

When we pray the Rosary on Thursdays, we think about events that happened after Jesus grew up and began to teach people about God his Father.

1. Jesus is baptized by his cousin John in the Jordan River.
2. Jesus turns water into wine at a wedding party in the town of Cana.
3. Jesus teaches crowds of people about the Kingdom of God and calls everyone to turn their hearts to God.
4. Three of the apostles see Jesus shining with God's glory on Mount Tabor.
5. Jesus gives us his Body and Blood, the Holy Eucharist, at the Last Supper.

The Sorrowful Mysteries

When we pray the Rosary on Tuesdays and Fridays, we think about the sufferings of Jesus—his passion and death on the cross.

1. In the Garden of Olives Jesus prays to his Father, saying: "Not my will but yours be done."
2. Jesus is condemned to death by the Roman governor Pontius Pilate. Pilate has Jesus whipped.
3. The soldiers place a painful crown of thorns on Jesus' head. Jesus bears this suffering with dignity.
4. Jesus sets out toward Calvary, carrying the heavy wood of the cross on his shoulders.
5. Jesus suffers and dies on the cross to show his great love for us and make it possible for us to be happy in heaven for ever.

The Glorious Mysteries

When we pray the Rosary on Wednesdays and Sundays, we think about the way Jesus overcame death by rising from the dead. We call this rising his *resurrection*.

1. After three days, Jesus rises from the dead by the power of God the Father. This shows that Jesus is God's dearly beloved Son.
2. Jesus goes up to heaven, where he sits at the right hand of the Father.
3. Jesus sends the Spirit of his love on the Church.
4. Mary is taken up into heaven body and soul and is welcomed by God, the angels, and the saints.
5. Mary is made queen of heaven. In heaven she prays to God for us, her children.

Hail, Holy Queen

Hail, holy Queen, Mother of mercy,
hail, our life, our sweetness, and our
　　hope.
To you we cry, the children of Eve;
to you we send up our sighs,
mourning and weeping in this land
　　of exile.
Turn, then, most gracious advocate,
your eyes of mercy toward us;
lead us home at last
and show us the blessed fruit of your
　　womb, Jesus:
O clement, O loving, O sweet Virgin
　　Mary.

A Short Prayer to Mary

We come to you for help,
holy Mother of God.
Please hear our prayers.
Save us from anything that could
　　hurt us,
glorious and blessed Virgin.

The Liturgica[l]

The Church's special year is called the *liturgical year*. It helps us to remember the events in the life of Jesus.

The liturgical year is divided into seasons and times instead of months. It begins with the First Sunday of Advent.

In the liturgical year we remember and celebrate everything God has done for us.

Year

The Season of Advent

We prepare to celebrate Jesus' birth.

"Advent" means a "coming," an "arrival."
Advent lasts four weeks.

During this time we remember what God
did to prepare the world to welcome
his Son, Jesus.

During Advent we can pray to the Lord like this:

Show me what I should do
to please you, Lord.
Teach me how to act.

Help me to live according to your truth.
Be my teacher,
because you are God, my Savior.

The Lord is good and honest.
He shows sinners the right way to live.

The Lord leads lowly people,
showing them the right things to do;
he teaches them his way.

Everything the Lord does is full of love
    for us.
He will always be faithful to us.
Lord, I think about you and love you.

Based on Psalm 25

The Seasons of Christmas and Epiphany

We celebrate because Jesus is born.

The Christmas-Epiphany Season begins on December 25. We celebrate Jesus' birth and the first times he showed himself to the world, especially through the Wise Men.

With the words of this Psalm, we join people all over the earth in thanking God the Father for the gift of his Son, Jesus:

Sing to the Lord a new song;
Let the whole world sing to the Lord and
    praise his name.
Every day tell about the way the Lord
    has saved us.
Talk about his glory and the wonderful
    things
he does to all the people on earth.
The Lord is great. He deserves our
    praise.
He is the only God. He made the whole
    universe.
Let us give to the Lord glory and praise.

Based on Psalm 96

Christmas Today

Every time I help someone in need,
I celebrate the birth of Jesus.
Every time I smile at someone who is
    sad,
I celebrate the birth of Jesus.
Every time I give someone my love,
I celebrate the birth of Jesus.

I can have Christmas every day!

The Season of Lent

We think, in a special way, about becoming more like Jesus.

Lent is the time of forty days that leads us to the special days of Holy Thursday, Good Friday, and Easter.
It is a time in which the Church encourages us to try harder to live the Gospel of Jesus.

During Lent we may say this prayer often:

Have mercy on me, God,
because you love me.
Wipe away all my sins.
Remove any guilt from me.
I know I have not always been good.
If you wash my sins away, I will be
    whiter than snow.
Give me a new heart that is full of love
    for you.
Make me happy by reminding me that
    you have saved me.
Help me to be strong and good.

*Based on
Psalm 51*

Holy Week

In this week just before the celebration of
Easter, we think about the last days in
the life of Jesus.
We remember his joyful entry into
Jerusalem, the institution of the
Eucharist, and Jesus' suffering and
death on the cross.

Special Days

On Holy Thursday

the Church helps us to remember the Last Supper, which Jesus had with his friends.

Jesus offered us his body and his blood as food and drink.

He did this to make our love for him and for one another grow stronger.

And Jesus said: "Do this in memory of me."

On Good Friday

we remember the way Jesus suffered and died for us.

On Holy Saturday

we quietly think about the great mystery of God's love for us.

God our Father did not hesitate to give us his own Son even though we were sinners.

The Stations of the Cross

The prayer called the *Stations of the Cross* reminds us that Jesus loves us so much that he died so that we could live with him in heaven some day. It's also a way for us to tell Jesus that we love him.

The "stations" are the small crosses you might see on the walls of your church. They usually have pictures with them. The pictures show different things that happened to Jesus as he was on his way to die for us. When you pray, imagine that you are walking with Jesus. If you are in church, you can walk from station to station.

Before you read the prayer for each station, say:

We adore you, O Christ, and we bless you.
Because by your holy cross, you have redeemed the world.

1. Jesus Is Condemned to Death

Jesus, your enemies wanted to kill you, even though you had done nothing wrong.
I pray for those who cause others to suffer.

2. Jesus Takes Up His Cross

Jesus, you loved us so much
that you were willing to carry the heavy
cross.
Help those who are in pain to remember
that you are always with them.

3. Jesus Falls the First Time

Jesus, it must have been very hard
for you to get up after falling.
Please be with me when I am having a
hard time being good.

4. Jesus Meets His Mother

Jesus, Mary wanted to be near you,
even though it made her sad to see you
suffering.
Please give me a love that is strong
enough
to comfort those who are suffering.

5. Simon of Cyrene Helps Jesus

Jesus, I think Simon probably did not
    want to help you at first.
Maybe later he was glad he had done it.
Help me to use every chance I have to be
    kind to others.

6. Veronica Wipes Jesus' Face

Jesus, Veronica was very brave and kind.
She wanted to comfort you,
and she didn't worry about what people
    thought of her.
I pray for all those who give their time to
    help others.

7. Jesus Falls the Second Time

Jesus, when you fell again,
you must have wondered if anyone
    would help you.

Please be with all people who are
   discouraged
and need someone to help them.

8. Jesus Meets the Kind Women

Jesus, these women were crying for you
in the middle of a crowd that was yelling
   and laughing at you.
Help all mothers, especially those whose
   families have problems.

9. Jesus Falls the Third Time

Jesus, it must have been so hard—
   almost impossible—
for you to get up and keep going.
Please free people who are addicted to
   alcohol or drugs.

10. Jesus' Clothes Are Torn Off

Jesus, how embarrassing this must have
    been for you.
I pray for all those who live in poverty
and who are ashamed that they don't
    have the clothes and food they need.

11. Jesus Is Nailed to the Cross

Jesus, how much it must have hurt you
    to be crucified!
Please be with all the people who are
    hurting inside
from loneliness or from feeling unloved.

12. Jesus Dies on the Cross

Jesus, as you were dying on the cross,
you prayed to your Father, and you
    thought of us with love.
I pray for all those who have died.

13. Jesus Is Taken Down from the Cross

Jesus, it was very painful for your mother
and your friends to see you dead.
Please comfort those who are sad
    because someone they love has died.

14. Jesus Is Laid in the Tomb

Jesus, when you were buried in the cave,
your friends were afraid that they would
    never see you again.
Help all those who live in fear. Let them
    know that you are close to them.

15. Jesus Rises from the Dead

Jesus, you were raised from death to
    new life.
May all Christians live the new life
that they have received through their
    baptism.

The Season of Easter–Pentecost

We joyfully tell everyone that Jesus Christ is risen.

For us Christians, Easter is the feast of the Risen Lord.

It is the most important celebration of the year.

Thanks to Jesus, we have been freed from sin.

His Spirit makes us live a new life.

Easter

Be happy with Christians all over the world and pray this beautiful hymn:

Alleluia, alleluia, alleluia!
Be glad angels and saints of heaven!

Let everyone and everything God
has created
celebrate around his throne!
Jesus Christ, our King, is risen!
Easter is the special feast when Jesus,
the Lamb of God,
has freed us from our sins.
Jesus, the light of the world, has
destroyed the darkness of sin.
Jesus has made us his special friends.
He has made us a family in the love of
God the Father.
We celebrate because the Church, our
Mother,
gives birth to her children in the waters
of baptism
and the Spirit of Jesus.
God our Father,
may the glowing candle we hold in
church on Easter
never lose its brightness.
Let its light show us the way to Jesus,
your Son,
who is risen from the dead and lives and
reigns for ever and ever.
Amen. Alleluia, alleluia, alleluia!

Pentecost

Fifty days after the feast of Easter,
God sent the Holy Spirit upon the apostles,
the same Spirit we receive on the day of
our baptism.
The Holy Spirit helps us to understand and
live the words of Jesus.

Before doing anything important,
ask the Holy Spirit to help you to do it in
the best way possible.

Prayer to the Holy Spirit

Come, Holy Spirit,
fill the hearts of your faithful people.
Make the fire of your love burn in us.
Come and make all creation new.

Hymn to the Holy Spirit
Holy Spirit, God of Love,
Come, and send us from above,
Rays of your own pure light.
Come, Father of those in need,

Come, rewarding every deed,
You are the light of our hearts.
You are the one who best consoles,
You are the welcome Guest of souls,
You give us peace and rest.
You help us when our work is hard,
You stay with us, as light, as guard,
You comfort us when we are sad.
Light immortal! Light divine!
Come into our hearts and shine,
Fill us with your holiness.
If you take your grace away,
Nothing good in us will stay.
Make us more and more like Jesus.
Heal our weakness, make us good.
Let our love grow as it should,
Wash away the wrong we do.
Keep all stubbornness far away
From all we do and all we say,
Let us follow where you lead us.
Keep us faithful to God's teachings
Fill us with your special blessings,
Gifts worth more than we can know.
Reward your people when they die
Give them life with you on high
Give them joys which never end.
Amen.

BOOKS & MEDIA

The Daughters of St. Paul operate book and media centers at the following addresses. Visit, call or write the one nearest you today, or find us on the World Wide Web, www.pauline.org

CALIFORNIA

3908 Sepulveda Blvd, Culver City, CA 90230 310-397-8676

2640 Broadway Street, Redwood City, CA 94063 650-369-4230

5945 Balboa Avenue, San Diego, CA 92111 858-565-9181

FLORIDA

145 S.W. 107th Avenue, Miami, FL 33174 305-559-6715

HAWAII

1143 Bishop Street, Honolulu, HI 96813 808-521-2731

Neighbor Islands call: 866-521-2731

ILLINOIS

172 North Michigan Avenue, Chicago, IL 60601 312-346-4228

LOUISIANA

4403 Veterans Memorial Blvd, Metairie, LA 70006 504-887-7631

MASSACHUSETTS

885 Providence Hwy, Dedham, MA 02026 781-326-5385

MISSOURI

9804 Watson Road, St. Louis, MO 63126 314-965-3512

NEW JERSEY

561 U.S. Route 1, Wick Plaza, Edison, NJ 08817 732-572-1200

NEW YORK

150 East 52nd Street, New York, NY 10022 212-754-1110

PENNSYLVANIA

9171-A Roosevelt Blvd, Philadelphia, PA 19114 215-676-9494

SOUTH CAROLINA

243 King Street, Charleston, SC 29401 843-577-0175

TENNESSEE

4811 Poplar Avenue, Memphis, TN 38117 901-761-2987

TEXAS

114 Main Plaza, San Antonio, TX 78205 210-224-8101

VIRGINIA

1025 King Street, Alexandria, VA 22314 703-549-3806

CANADA

3022 Dufferin Street, Toronto, ON M6B 3T5 416-781-9131

¡También somos su fuente para libros, videos y música en español!